DEC   2012

Ripley's Believe It or Not!®

Developed and produced by Ripley Publishing Ltd

This edition published and distributed by:

Mason Crest
370 Reed Road, Broomall, Pennsylvania 19008
www.masoncrest.com

Printed and bound in the United States of America.

First printing
9 8 7 6 5 4 3 2 1

Ripley's Believe It or Not!
The Last Word
ISBN-13: 978-1-4222-2571-4 (hardcover)
ISBN-13: 978-1-4222-9246-4 (e-book)
Ripley's Believe It or Not!—Complete 16 Title Series
ISBN-13: 978-1-4222-2560-8

Library of Congress Cataloging-in-Publication Data

The last word.
    p. cm. — (Ripley's believe it or not!)
ISBN 978-1-4222-2571-4 (hardcover) — ISBN 978-1-4222-2560-8 (series hardcover) —
ISBN 978-1-4222-9246-4 (ebook)
 1. Curiosities and wonders--Juvenile literature.
 AG243.P74 2012
 031.02—dc23
                            2012020384

PUBLISHER'S NOTE
While every effort has been made to verify the accuracy of the entries in this book, the Publisher's cannot be held responsible for any errors contained in the work. They would be glad to receive any information from readers.

WARNING
Some of the stunts and activities in this book are undertaken by experts and should not be attempted by anyone without adequate training and supervision.

Disbelief and Shock!

THE LAST WORD

www.MasonCrest.com

THE LAST WORD

Out of this world. Lose yourself in this book

of mind-boggling science, fantastic food, and

remarkable inventions. Read about the armchairs

you can race in, the egg that times itself so it

is always boiled to perfection, and the robot

that can play the violin.

This two-seater watercraft looks and behaves like a real dolphin.

Among Jason's pencil designs is a sparkling golden arrow on the ceiling.

The stairs lead up from a Victorian parlor, so Jason copied the design of an original Victorian wallpaper pattern in the stairwell—in pencils, of course.

Pencil-Vania

Jason also created a face made of pencils—a futuristic portrait of Jaina aged 88.

A garden scene of flowers and peeping sprites is another of the mosaic's special features.

Inside a San Francisco house, artist Jason Mecier has created a wonderful, colorful mosaic from thousands of pencils. He calls it Pencil-Vania.

When Jason's friend Jaina Davis bought the 100-year-old property on Potrero Hill, San Francisco, in 1997, she invited her artist friends to design the interior. Jason conceived the idea of connecting the styles of the different rooms by a pencil mosaic winding up the staircase, and was commissioned to create just that. As a result, doors, banisters, and walls have all been decorated with brightly colored pencils that have been glued to the surfaces, inserted in specially drilled holes, or suspended from the ceiling.

Jason's amazing mosaic includes a pencil flower garden, pencil Victorian-style wallpaper, and a futuristic pencil portrait of Jaina, aged 88.

Work in progress on one of the stairwell walls.

Pencil-Vania includes shelves made from pencils, many of which are home to a variety of office supplies.

Ripley's ask

"

How would you describe Pencil-Vania? Pencil-Vania—the "Forest of Pencils"—is a mixed media art installation in the three-story stairwell of the private home of Jaina Davis in San Francisco, California. The installation, which I designed and fitted myself, covers the walls, banisters, ceilings, molding, trim, shelves, and three doors from the first floor, up two landings, and all the way to the top of the third floor. That's 980 square feet plus 20 feet of handrails.

How many pencils are there? According to our calculations, there are 92,626.

How long did it take to create? Five years, from 1997 to 2002.

How much did it cost? $50,000.

Where did all the pencils come from? The bulk of the pencils were purchased from two local reuse centers. Others were ordered from office- and school-supply catalogs, and because the house is located between two schools, Jaina would pick up abandoned pencils on her daily excursions. She also held a garage sale that accepted no money in exchange for goods—only pencils. Sometimes boxes of pencils were even left anonymously on the doorstep.

Is there anything other than pencils in the installation? There are erasers, pencil sharpeners, a renegade pen or two, and a few assorted office supplies—staplers, rulers, compasses, scissors. There's also a huge rubber-band ball on the banister.

What inspired this unusual idea? I visited Grandma Prisbrey's Bottle Village in California as a child and learned folk arts and crafts from my own grandmother. Jaina had always loved unusual homes and dreamed that one day she would live in one of her very own.

What's it like for Jaina living within walls of pencils? She says it smells like the first day of school every day!

"

VACUUM SHOES

A new pair of shoes has been invented that vacuums as you walk. The "Shoover" has a tiny rechargeable vacuum cleaner inside the base that collects dust while the wearer walks around the house.

THIN SET

The Japanese company Sony unveiled a new flat-screen television set in 2007 that is about the same width as a coin.

LIGHT MOVERS

All electrons and protons moving through the wires, cables, and transistors of the Internet have a combined weight of less than 2 oz (57 g).

THINK SMALL

Korean nanotechnology researchers used lasers and microscopic materials to create a copy of Rodin's sculpture *The Thinker* that is only twice the size of a red blood cell.

BELT CONVENTION

The Niagara Aerospace Museum in Niagara Falls, New York, holds an annual convention dedicated to rocket belts—jet packs that can propel a person into the air.

ROBOT FLY

Scientists at Harvard University have created a life-size robotic fly. Weighing only 0.002 oz (60 milligrams) with a wingspan of $1^3/_{16}$ in (3 cm), the minute robot's movements are modeled on those of a real fly. It is hoped that the mechanical insects might one day be used as spies or for detecting dangerous chemicals.

INVINCIBLE OPPONENT

Computer scientists at the University of Alberta, Canada, have created a program for playing checkers that cannot be beaten. The program's name is Chinook.

ROBOTIC VIOLINIST

A Japanese company has built a robot that can actually play the violin. Created by the Toyota Motor Corporation, the 5-ft-tall (1.5-m) robot has 17 joints in its hands and arms to give it human-like dexterity. At the product launch, it used its mechanical fingers to push the strings correctly while bowing with its other arm to give a near-perfect rendition of Edward Elgar's "Pomp and Circumstance."

DOUBLE VISION

Zou Renti introduces his robot twin at a conference on intelligent robots and systems in Beijing, China. To make it appear more human, the robot has a lifelike skin made of silica gel. In case you're still not sure, the robot is the one on the right.

BIONIC HAND

Born without the lower part of her left arm, Lindsay Block of Oklahoma City, Oklahoma, demonstrates her new i-LIMB bionic hand—a prosthetic device that looks and works like a human hand. It has individually powered fingers that can grip objects and works via small electrodes taped to the skin of the wearer's forearm, which transmit signals to tiny electric motors that power the false hand's movements.

SWELL IDEA
Scientists in Naples, Italy, have invented a new weight-loss pill that swells up to the size of a tennis ball in the stomach. The pill, which is made out of diaper material, makes people feel full for about two hours.

EYE TEST
English scientist Sir Isaac Newton (1643–1727) once slid a needle into his eye socket to create spots in his vision so he could study the results for an optics experiment.

SLOW START
Invented by King Camp Gillette, the safety razor first went on sale in the United States in 1903, but only 51 were sold in the first 12 months. In 1904, Gillette sold 90,000!

ROBOT RESCUE
The U.S. Army is developing a robot that can carry a wounded soldier from a battlefield. BEAR (Battlefield Extraction-Assist Robot) can lift more than 300 lb (135 kg) and is able to climb stairs holding a human-sized dummy.

TALKING PLANTS
New York University students have invented a device whereby plants that need watering telephone their owners for help. Activated by moisture sensors placed in the soil, the plant sends a signal of "I'm thirsty" over a wireless communication network. When the owner answers the call, the plant's "voice" (an audio file) relays the problem. The plant also calls back after being watered to say "Thank you." Each type of plant is given a different recorded voice to match its biological traits.

MOUSE IN A MOUSE ~~~

Americans Christy Canida and Noah Weinsrein created a computer mouse housed inside a real mouse! They used the skin of a dead rodent bought from a pet shop.

CAFFEINE RUSH ~~~

U.S. firm Think Geek has manufactured a soap that releases caffeine into the user's system, providing the same energizing effect as two cups of coffee. Shower Shock is designed for people who do not have time for both a shower and a cup of coffee in their morning routine.

ARCTIC STUDY ~~~

Kristin Laidre, a researcher at the University of Washington, studies the depths of inaccessible parts of the Arctic Ocean by strapping scientific instruments to narwhals.

TRAINED BEES ~~~

Honeybees are being used to help find unexploded landmines in Croatia. Scientists at Zagreb University have been training the bees to locate explosive chemicals using the bees' keen sense of smell. The bees are trained to associate the smell of explosives with food so they settle on ground where mines are buried.

SPECIAL GOATS ~~~

A U.S. biotech company breeds goats that produce a nerve gas antidote in their milk.

LIGHT-BOILED EGG ~~~

English inventor Simon Rhymes from Chippenham, Wiltshire, has devised a machine that boils the perfect egg, using lightbulbs instead of water. The eggs are lowered into the machine and heated by four halogen bulbs. After cooking the egg, the gadget even slices off the top so that bread can be dipped into the yolk.

COOL FOR CATS ~~~

Nohl Rosen of Scottsdale, Arizona, runs a web radio station for cats that features interviews with veterinarians and pet owners, plus music approved by cats. The station manager of Cat Galaxy is Rosen's own cat Isis (she loves funk and Ozzy Osbourne). Her assistant and the station's program director are also cats.

INSPIRED BY NATURE ~~~

Scientists from Northwestern University, Evanston, Illinois, have created a new super-sticky material based on the natural adhesive powers of geckos and mussels. The material, called "geckel," is effective because it is made from coating fibrous silicone—a substance similar in structure to a gecko's foot—with a polymer that replicates the powerful "glue" used by mussels.

PIGEON CONTROL ~~~

Scientists in Shandong, China, have learned to control the flight of pigeons by implanting electrodes in the birds' brains. The researchers have designed a computer system that allows them to instruct the pigeons to fly left, right, up, or down.

Here, the cat on the right has the "fluorescent" gene and will glow under ultraviolet light, whereas the cat on the left does not.

The altered skin color of the "glow-in-the-dark" cat is clearly seen here—on the ears and nose, compared with the unaltered cat on the left.

Scientists in South Korea have created cats that glow red. Researchers at Gyeongsang National University manipulated a gene in two cloned white Turkish Angora cats to change the cats' skin color so that they would have a fluorescent glow under ultraviolet light.

GLOWING CATS

ALBINO BIRTH

At Jamestown, North Dakota, in 2007, White Cloud, North America's only female albino bison, gave birth to an albino calf, named Dakota Miracle. The chances of this happening naturally in the wild would be one in ten million!

ANT INTELLIGENCE

Scientists from the University of Bristol, England, have observed that army ants form living bridges to help get jobs done. When ants are foraging on rough ground, some of them use their own bodies to plug tiny holes and allow their fellow ants to walk over them. It was even discovered that individual ants choose which of them is the best size to lie across a particular hole.

HOMEMADE REACTOR

Thiago Olson, a 17-year-old high school student from Oakland Township, Michigan, built a functioning fusion reactor in his garage. It took him two years and more than 1,000 hours of research.

THE BEST MEDICINE

Scientists from Vanderbilt University in Nashville, Tennessee, believe that laughing for 15 minutes a day can help people lose weight. They say daily laughter can burn off up to 5 lb (2.3 kg) of fat a year.

ZOMBIE DOGS

In trials to develop suspended animation for humans, scientists in the United States have managed to bring dead dogs back to life. The Safar Center for Resuscitation Research in Pittsburgh, Pennsylvania, rendered the dogs clinically dead by draining their veins of blood and replacing it with an ice-cold salt solution. The animals stopped breathing, but three hours later they were revived with no ill effects after their blood was put back.

RAMPANT RAT

A prehistoric skull found in a museum in Montevideo, Uruguay, has led scientists to conclude that a rodent the size of a cow roamed the forests of South America four million years ago. The monster rat stood 5 ft (1.5 m) tall, was 10 ft (3 m) long and weighed almost a ton, making it 14 times bigger than any rodent alive today.

BARK ANALYSIS

Hungarian scientists have developed computer software that will enable humans to understand dog barks. Following the analysis of 6,000 barks, the amazing software can differentiate between a dog's various barks to be able to tell when it has seen a ball, when it meets a stranger, or when it wants to be taken for a walk.

FEARLESS MICE

Scientists at Japan's Tokyo University have created a mouse that is not scared of cats. The researchers succeeded in turning off the receptors in a mouse's brain that react to the scent of its chief predator. The result has been the creation of genetically modified mice who show no fear when coming face-to-face with cats.

SEE-THROUGH FROG!

Scientists in Japan have bred transparent frogs whose organs, blood vessels, and eggs can be seen clearly through their skins. Experts say the frogs will be invaluable for research into diseases such as cancer, because scientists can study organ growth and development without having to dissect the frog... which is good news for the frog, too.

PRICE OF LOVE

A Japanese chocolate made for Valentine's Day 2006 was encrusted with 2,006 diamonds and priced at 500 million yen ($4.4 million). The chocolate was designed in the shape of the continent of Africa.

TINY SUSHI
Sushi on single tiny grains of rice is served at the Omoroi Sushiya Kajiki Sushi Restaurant in Fukuoka, Japan.

LARGE SLAB
In May 2007, the Northwest Fudge Factory of Levack, Ontario, Canada, produced a slab of fudge that measured 45½ ft (13.9 m) long, 6½ ft (2 m) wide, and 4 in (10 cm) thick, and weighed 5,038 lb (2,285 kg).

SCOTCH GEORGE
George Washington, the first president of the United States, also ran one of the largest whiskey distilleries in North America.

COLOR CHANGE
The first orange carrot was bred by Dutch farmers to honor their royal family, the House of Orange. Prior to that, most carrots were purple, yellow, or white.

EXPENSIVE TASTE

A hamburger on the menu at the Ritz-Carlton Hotel in Tokyo, Japan, costs 13,450 yen ($112)—that's more than 40 times the price of a McDonald's burger. The beef in the burger comes from Wagyu cattle, which are specially bred for the flavor, juiciness, and tenderness of their meat. ▽

LUXURY BAGEL ▲

Frank Tujague, executive chef of the Westin New York Hotel in Times Square, prepared a $1,000 bagel in 2007. Topped with white truffle cream-cheese and goji berry-infused Riesling jelly with golden leaves, the luxury bagel was so pricey because white truffle is the second most expensive food in the world, next to premium caviar.

GOLDEN DESSERT △

In 2007, a New York City restaurant unveiled a chocolate dessert costing a cool $25,000. Stephen Bruce, owner of Serendipity 3, revealed that the expensive sundae contained a blend of 28 rare cocoas from 14 countries, topped with cream and sprinkled with 23-carat edible gold dust and an exotic truffle. In addition to the food, the customer got to take home the gold-and-diamond goblet in which it was served, the 18-carat gold spoon used to eat it, and a ladies' gold bracelet.

GIANT OMELETTE

Sixty thousand eggs were poured into a specially built 44-ft (13.4-m) pan to make a giant omelette weighing 6,510 lb (2,950 kg) at Brockville, Ontario, Canada in 2002.

CAKE CATHEDRAL

George D'Aubney built a 4-ft-tall (1.2-m) replica of the famous landmark St. Paul's Cathedral in London, England. The replica was complete with lights, music, moving parts—and made primarily from fruitcake.

BANANA SPLITS

There are more than 300 banana-related accidents a year in Britain, most involving people slipping on skins.

RICH DESSERT

A restaurant in the Sri Lankan resort of Galle is charging $14,500 for a dessert, which comes with a chocolate sculpture and a large gemstone. The Fortress Stilt Fisherman Indulgence consists of cassata, mango, pomegranate, champagne, and an 80-carat aquamarine stone.

SOUND OF THE SEA

At his restaurant in Berkshire, England, chef Heston Blumenthal serves a dish that comes with an iPod Nano in a clamshell—so that customers can listen to the sea as they eat their seafood.

POPCORN BALL

A popcorn ball that measured 8 ft (2.4 m) in diameter and 24½ ft (7.5 m) in circumference and weighed 3,415 lb (1,150 kg) was manufactured at Lake Forest, Illinois, in October 2006.

COFFEE SENTENCE

King Gustav III, who ruled Sweden in the 18th century, was so convinced that coffee was poisonous that he ordered a convicted criminal to drink himself to death with it. However, the condemned man eventually died of old age instead.

POTATO FIGHT

In 2007, a woman in Nicholson, Georgia, knocked out her husband with a potato! She picked up the potato and threw it at him during a row and it hit him square on the nose. He decided not to press charges.

Prized Lychee

Known as the "king of fruit," the lychee has always been popular in China. Few, however, have been sold for anything like the price of this one, which went for a huge 555,000 yuan ($67,000) at auction in Zengcheng City, China, in 2002. It came from a 400-year-old tree, named Xiyuangualu, which yields only a few dozen lychees each year.

FLYING HOVERCRAFT

An inventor from New Zealand has devised a hovercraft with wings that flies 6 ft (1.8 m) above the water. Rudy Heeman has spent 11 years designing the Hoverwing, a two-passenger vehicle with an ability to lift off that leaves other water-based craft in its wake. It sets off like an ordinary hovercraft but on reaching its top speed of 60 mph (97 km/h), its wings can be extended, enabling it to take to the air.

算 算 数

8 + 2 = 10

4 = 5

X3 = 9

-5 = 2

SPEED SURFER

A Swedish pensioner is able to surf the Internet many thousands of times faster than anybody else in the world, thanks to a connection installed by her son. Seventy-five-year-old Sigbritt Lothberg of Karlstad has a 40-gigabits-per-second connection, so she can download a full-length movie in less than two seconds.

SOCK RIDDLE

The Bureau of Missing Socks is the first website devoted exclusively to solving the riddle of what happens to single missing socks—with explanations from the occult to aliens.

IMAGINARY FRIEND

A man from Newport, Wales, who tried to sell his imaginary friend on eBay in 2007 attracted bids of more than $3,000. The seller, calling himself "thewildandcrazyoli," decided to sell his pretend friend, Jon Malipieman, because at 27, he had grown out of him.

PEANUT GEMS

Scientists at the University of Edinburgh, Scotland, say they can turn peanut butter into diamonds. They claim that the carbon in peanut butter can be transformed into precious gems by subjecting it to pressures of five million atmospheres—that's higher than the pressure found at the center of the Earth.

COUNTING CHICKEN

A hen in Shenyang, China, can apparently do simple arithmetic. The bird's owner says the chicken can peck the answer to simple calculations when he points to numbers on a board and asks her questions. She also knows and can point to the 26 letters of the alphabet when asked to do so.

SEARCH DEVICE

Police in Strathclyde, Scotland, have introduced an Unmanned Airborne Vehicle (UAV) to help search for missing people. The lightweight portable device is able to carry out searches using photography and video, its advantage being that it can be safely flown in weather conditions that prevent traditional aircraft from leaving the ground.

GIANT COIN

A 220-lb (100-kg) gold coin the size of a pizza was produced by the Royal Canadian Mint in 2007. Worth $2 million, the coin featured maple leaves on one side and Queen Elizabeth II on the other.

ELECTRIC CHARGE

Human sweat is able to create an electrical charge in coins that have two different alloys—like the Canadian Toonie or the 1 and 2 euro coins.

CONVERTED CART

Bill Lauver of Middleburg, Pennsylvania, converted an electric golf cart into a remote-controlled snowplow so that he could clear his driveway of snow from the comfort of his living room.

TRUTH GLASSES

A New York company has brought out a pair of sunglasses that can tell whether people are speaking the truth. The lie detector eyeglasses can monitor conversations in real-time and provide an LED display of the truthfulness of people around the wearer with 95 percent accuracy.

MULTI-TASK TOILET

The prize in a 2007 contest held by a U.S. plumbing company was an HDTV, DVD player, game system, laptop computer, digital music player, exercise machine, cooling fan, and refrigerator—all connected to a toilet.

PHONE CHANTS

To raise funds, Brazil's Xavante tribe records traditional chants for cell-phone ringtones.

DISCARDED GEAR

A North American website shows pictures of clothing that have been discarded on sidewalks across the world. These include T-shirts, sneakers, baseball caps, and even a prosthetic leg in Singapore.

BEER LAUNCH

A student from North Carolina has invented a refrigerator that throws cold cans of beer to drinkers. John Cornwell spent $3,000 devising the Beer Launching Fridge, which, when activated by remote control, rotates an arm to line itself up with its target and then catapults the can up to 10 ft (3 m) away.

SOLAR HEATING

A Chinese farmer obtains hot water from a device made of beer bottles connected by lengths of hosepipe. Ma Yanjun from Shaanxi Province, has attached 66 beer bottles to a board on the roof of his house. Sunlight heats the water as it passes slowly through the bottles and it eventually flows into his bathroom as hot water.

CANNED BURGER

A Swiss firm has invented a cheeseburger in a can. The burger is meant for hikers, who have to heat the can in a water container over a fire for two minutes, and then eat.

ROBOT WAITER

Japanese engineers have invented a robot 3 ft 8 in (1.2 m) tall that can serve breakfast. Called Twendy-One, the robot has long arms and 241 pressure sensors in each hand, enabling it to perform such chores as picking up a loaf of bread without crushing it, putting toast on a plate, and fetching ketchup from a refrigerator.

QUICK CHANGE

A new invention means that women can now switch from flats to stilettos without having to change shoes. The shoes have a retractable high heel that disappears when driving, but then extends again at the push of a button.

SLEEP EASY

Designers in the U.K. have developed a pair of pajamas that regulate body temperature to help the wearer enjoy a good night's sleep. Made from a special material, the invention follows research showing that a person's body temperature changes constantly throughout the night, affecting his or her sleep pattern.

PERFECT EGG

Scientists in Britain have developed an egg that times itself so it is always boiled to perfection. Choosing from cartons labeled "soft," "medium," or "hard," shoppers buy eggs that are marked with lion logos in heat-sensitive invisible ink. The ink turns black as soon as the egg is ready—this takes from three minutes for soft-boiled to seven minutes for hard-boiled.

LATTE ART

Visitors to a café in Melbourne, Australia, often find a face, a flower, or a butterfly staring back at them from the cup. The artistic frothy designs are all the rage among the city's baristas who use the coffee cup as a canvas and even take part in special latte art competitions. The patterns are created either by manipulating the flow of milk from a jug into an espresso or by etching, using stencils, powders, and milk foam.

GIANT KEBAB

Using 3.8 tons of chicken meat, 250 students in Cyberjaya, Malaysia, created a kebab that was more than 1¼ mi (2 km) long.

LUXURY PIZZA

Domenico Crolla, a chef from Glasgow, Scotland, creates a specialty pizza with a $4,000 price tag. It includes champagne-soaked caviar, cognac-marinated lobster, smoked salmon, venison, and 24-carat edible gold shavings. It is named the Pizza Royale 007 after James Bond.

TEA BAG

In 2006, a German company made a tea bag that was 11 x 8½ ft (3.4 x 2.6 m). It contained more than 22 lb (10 kg) of tea.

ULTIMATE TAKEOUT

An Indian restaurant in Belfast, Northern Ireland, delivered the ultimate takeout meal in 2006—to Manhattan. Steve Francis, a New York dance music producer, ordered the $16,000 transatlantic takeout—complete with fish flown in specially from Bangladesh—after Arif Ahmed's Indie Spice restaurant had served him delicious food at a festival in England.

SUPER SOUP

Cooks in Caracas, Venezuela, prepared a 3,963-gal (15,000-l) pot of soup in September 2007 that was big enough to feed 70,000 people. The soup contained 6,615 lb (3,000 kg) of chicken, 4,410 lb (2,000 kg) of beef, and literally tons of vegetables.

SUNDAE BEST

In 1988, Mike Rogiani of Edmonton, Alberta, Canada, created an ice cream sundae that weighed a staggering 54,917 lb (24,910 kg). The ingredients—which included 63 different flavors of ice cream—cost about $7,000 and had to be mixed in an empty swimming pool.

BANANA BUNCH

A bunch of bananas harvested in Holguin, Cuba, in 2007, contained more than 300 bananas. The bunch was 3 ft 10 in (1.2 m) high and weighed 125 lb (57 kg). Amazingly, the plant was growing in a clay soil to which no fertilizers had been added—apparently, water was the only catalyst needed for such enormous growth.

STARBUCKS ADVENTURER

Poughkeepsie, NY

Seekonk, MA

Freeport, NY

Carmel, NY

Incline Village, NV

DRIP FEED

At a hospital-themed restaurant in Taipei, Taiwan, customers drink from intravenous tubes suspended from the ceiling. The waitresses are dressed as nurses, crutches hang from the walls, a wheelchair is parked in the lobby, and the sign for the bathrooms is marked "emergency room."

CHOCOLATE IGLOO

Marco Fanti and his co-workers created a 9,200-lb (4,173-kg) igloo totally out of edible chocolate for the Eurochocolate Fair in Perugia, Italy, in 2006.

CREAM CAKE

In Alanya, Turkey, 285 cooks baked a cream cake 8,840 ft (2,720 m) long, using 159,000 eggs, 12,150 lb (5,512 kg) of sugar, 12,150 lb (5,512 kg) of flour, 1,400 gal (5,300 l) of milk, 5,840 lb (2,650 kg) of bananas, 700 gal (2,650 l) of water, and 1,750 lb (795 kg) of carbonate and baking additives.

GOOD KARMA

Hoping to bring some good karma to his establishment, a restaurant owner in Guangdong, China, paid $75,000 for a single "lucky" fish in April 2007.

COLOSSAL CAKE

To celebrate the centennial of Las Vegas in May 2005, a giant birthday cake was baked that measured 102 ft (31 m) long, 52 ft (16 m) wide and 20 in (50 cm) high. It weighed 130,000 lb (59,000 kg), had 34,000 lb (15,420 kg) of icing, and contained 23 million calories!

MASSIVE MUG

In April 2007, a Panama coffee producer brewed a 750-gal (2,840-l) cup of coffee. Café Duran took four hours and used 300 lb (135 kg) of coffee to fill a 9-ft (2.7-m) tall mug.

DAIRY DELIGHT

Stew Leonard's, a family-owned foodstore with outlets in Connecticut and New York, has the world's largest in-store dairy plant, packaging more than 10 million half-gallon (2 l) cartons per year. That's enough milk to fill a straw reaching from Earth to the Moon and halfway back!

CHEESY HIT

More than 1.5 million people have logged on to an Internet site to watch a round of Cheddar cheese as it slowly matures in a storeroom in western England.

FROG FEAST

Visitors to the annual four-day Fellsmere Frog Leg Festival in Florida routinely eat around 6,000 lb (2,720 kg) of crispy fried frogs' legs.

For more than ten years, a contract computer programmer named Winter has been on a mission to drink a cup of coffee in every Starbucks store in the world. The idea originated in 1997 at his local Starbucks in Plano, Texas, and by October 2007 he had visited 7,103 stores in the United States (92.7 per cent of the total) and 457 international stores, from Montreal to Madrid and Paris to Hong Kong. Winter, whose travels are documented in the movie "Starbucking," started out averaging around ten stores a day, although in 1999 he managed 28 in one day at Portland, Oregon. The only problem is that Starbucks continues to open new stores every week around the world and has no plans to slow down!

Chicago, IL

East Wenatchee, WA

Edmonton, AB

Grand Rapids, MI

GIANT CALZONE

In 2007, a restaurant in Madison, Wisconsin, created a huge calzone pizza measuring 19 ft 4 in x 2 ft 5 in (5.9 x 0.74 m) and weighing more than 100 lb (45 kg).

LARGE TIP

A family who were regulars at a Pizza Hut restaurant in Angola, Indiana, were so impressed by their waitress that they gave her a $10,000 tip. After 20-year-old waitress Jessica Osborne had told them she had twice been forced to drop out of college because of lack of money, they returned a few days later with the surprise check.

GOING POP

More than 500 Canadian boy scouts popped over 1,200 cubic ft (34 cubic m) of popcorn in just eight hours in 2007. Using two giant, homemade machines, the scouts popped at an average rate of two cubic ft per minute into a large bucket at the Calgary Zoo, Alberta.

POPPADUM PILE

Richard Bradbury and Kris Browcott took four hours to stack a pile of around 1,000 poppadums to a height of nearly 5 ft (1.5 m) at an Indian restaurant in London, England.

SQUIRREL PANCAKES

A hotel in Cumbria, England, served up free gray squirrel pancakes. The squirrels were all caught in the grounds of the Famous Wild Boar Hotel at Crook and served in Peking duck-style wraps. Customers said the squirrel meat tasted like rabbit.

SOLO FEAST

A Thanksgiving meal for ten people was devoured by just one person in 15 minutes in 2007. Competitive eater Tim Janus from New York City consumed a 10-lb (4.5-kg) turkey, 4 lb (1.8 kg) of mashed potatoes, 3 lb (1.4 kg) of cranberry sauce, and 2½ lb (1.1 kg) of beans... and still had room for dessert—an entire pumpkin pie.

COSTLY TRUFFLE

A white truffle weighing 1 lb 10 oz (750 g) from Alba, Italy, was sold to a Hong Kong resident for $210,000 in 2007. Italian truffles were more expensive than usual in 2007 following a dry summer.

CHOPSTICK EXPERT

In November 2007, Rob Beaton of Asbury Park, New Jersey, used chopsticks to eat 78 single grains of rice in three minutes.

TEA DRINKER

Levi Johnson of Tea, South Dakota, drank 5½ oz (165 ml) of hot Tabasco® sauce—that's nearly three bottles—in just 30 seconds in 2007.

FISH HOOK

A man eating fish at a restaurant in Shanghai, China, got a fish hook stuck in his tongue. At first he thought it was a bone, but when he discovered blood all over his mouth, he was taken to a hospital where the hook was removed.

DIRT SODA

For its contract to supply soda to Qwest Field, home of the Seattle Seahawks football team, Jones Soda Co. came up with new flavors, such as Perspiration, Dirt, Sports Cream, and Natural Field Turf.

BIG BIRD

As part of an annual contest with his sister Andra to see who can cook the biggest Thanksgiving turkey, Rich Portnoy, of Minneapolis, Minnesota, basted a bird weighing 72 lb (33 kg). The giant turkey needed 15 hours of roasting in a 36-in-wide (90-cm) oven.

GINGERBREAD HOUSES

Some of the most beautiful buildings in the world are displayed each year at the Grove Park Inn, Asheville, North Carolina—and they're all made out of gingerbread. First staged in 1993, the National Gingerbread House Competition draws sugar-and-spice creations from all over the United States.

Valerie Enters created a fairytale crooked house for the 2006 competition.

Trish MacCallister took third prize with a festive gingerbread house in 2005.

Patricia Howard of Winter Springs, Florida, won the coveted Grand Prize with this snowy scene at the 2006 National Gingerbread Competition. She retained her title in 2007.

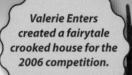

NICE ICE!

An ice-cream parlor in Nice, France, sells tomato-flavored sorbet. Fenocchio offers 70 beautifully presented flavors of ice cream and sorbet, including such wacky tastes as tomato and basil, black olive, rhubarb, lavender, and gingerbread.

Top Ten Unusual Ice Cream Flavors

Tomato & basil	Thyme
Black olive	Lavender
Licorice	Chewing gum
Beer	Violet
Rosemary	Rose

An enchanting gingerbread church won *Virginia Pilarz* third place in 2006.

A bejewelled gingerbread model of St. Basil's Cathedral in Moscow earned *Nancy Kyzer* first place at the 2005 contest.

FESTIVAL OF FIRE

To celebrate the feast of Saint Anthony (the patron saint of animals), horses and riders jump through burning pyres each January in the Spanish village of San Bartolomé de Pinares as part of the Las Luminarias de San Anton Festival. Cheered on by enthusiastic crowds, more than 100 horses and riders, some carrying small children, brave the flames from 30 bonfires laid out over the 0.6-mi (1-km) course. The controversial ceremony, which dates back hundreds of years, stems from the belief that running through fire will cleanse the village of disease.

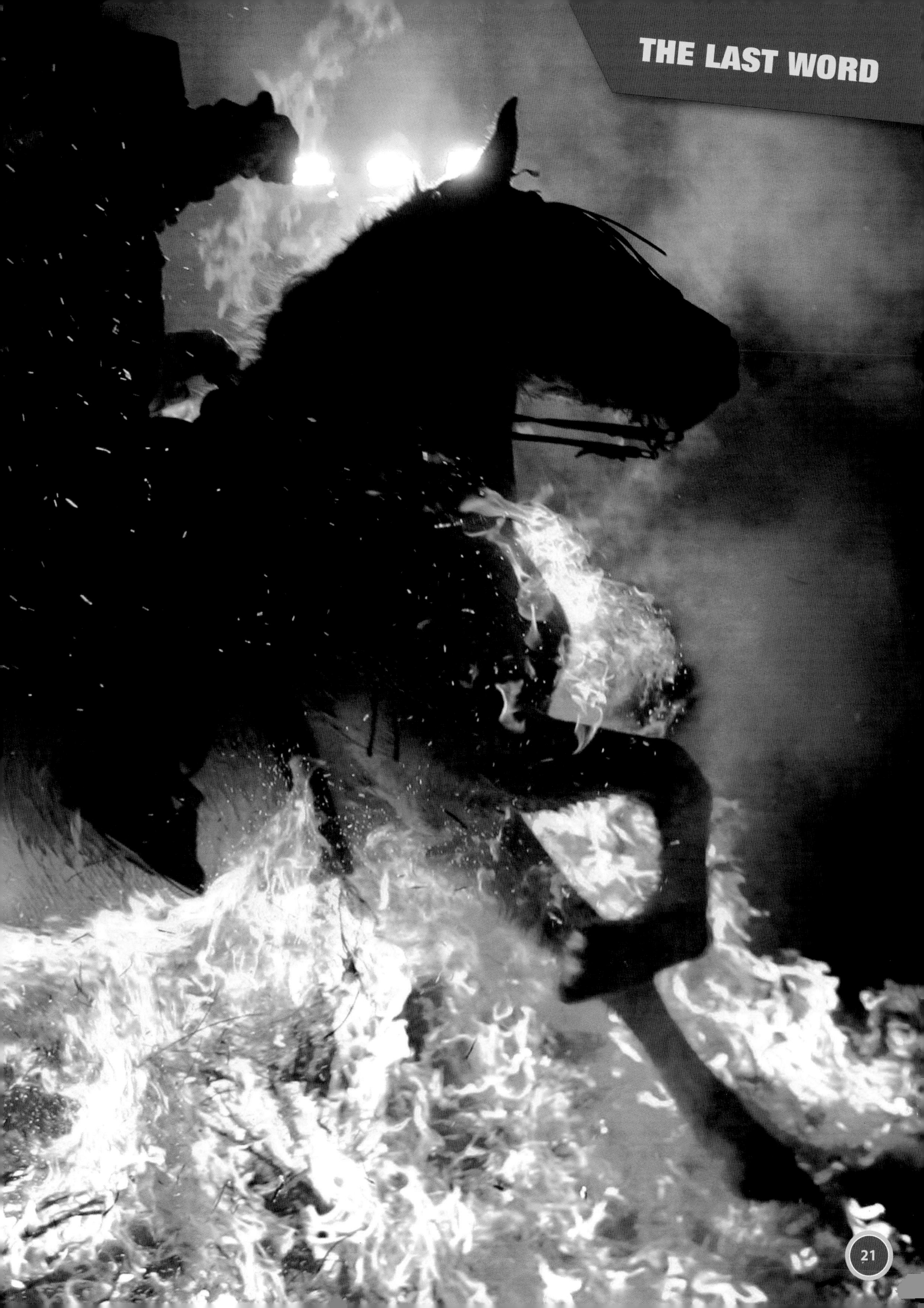

MARRIED HIMSELF

A narcissistic Chinese man married himself before 100 guests in Zhuhai City, China, in 2007. Liu Ye married a life-sized foam cut-out of himself wearing a woman's bridal dress.

SAME DRESS

In 2007, Charlotte Middleton of Norfolk, England, became the sixth bride in her family to wear the same wedding dress. The chiffon and satin gown was first worn by her great grandmother in 1910.

THE CORPSE GROOM

Tulsi Devipujak of Anand, Gujarat, India, married her fiancé, Sanjay Dantania, in March 2007 even though he died in an accident before the ceremony. The bride's family dressed the corpse like a groom and conducted the marriage rituals on a decorated stage.

SHE'S MINE!

A couple in Merioneth, Wales, proved just how deep their love was—by getting married 500 ft (152 m) below ground in an abandoned slate mine. Kerry Bevan and Wayne Davies and their 15 guests wore traditional wedding attire with the addition of helmets and gum boots.

BAD LUCK

Seventy-five-year-old Phulram Chaudhary of Nepal married a dog in a local custom to ensure good luck. The charm didn't work, as he died three days later!

LONG DRESS

A Chinese man had a 656-ft-long (200-m) wedding dress made for his fiancée. Ken, the groom from Guangzhou, originally intended to make the dress 2,008 m (1¼ mi) long in tribute to the 2008 Beijing Olympics, but decided to reduce it to 200.8 m (658 ft). It took nearly three months to make and weighed almost 220 lb (100 kg).

LOVE IS IN THE AIR

Two high-rise window cleaners were married hanging in the air on their work platforms while guests cheered some 50 ft (15 m) below. Jiang Dezhang and Tie Guangju tied the knot in Yunnan Province, China, in August 2007 while sitting on wooden boards supported by ropes and pulleys. The best man and bridesmaid were suspended alongside.

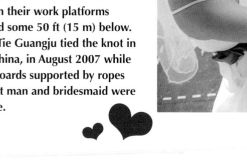

HEN-PECKED HUSBAND
At the wedding of Terry Morris and Renee Biwer near Bismarck, North Dakota, in August 2006, the bridesmaid was a chicken! Henrietta the hen has been a pet of the groom's for 12 years and even stays in hotel rooms with the couple. The ceremony had a distinct barnyard feel to it, with the bride and groom riding in on horseback and saying their vows from the saddle.

ARBOREAL BLISS
Believing the ritual would ward off evil spirits, hundreds of people gathered in English Bazaar, India, in December 2006, to witness a marriage ceremony between two trees.

DIVORCE GIFT
In October 2006, a man in Vienna, Austria, spitefully cut off his ring finger and presented it—complete with wedding band—to his ex-wife after their divorce became final.

DONUT NUPTIALS
In addition to creating pastries, the employees of the Voodoo Doughnut Shop of Portland, Oregon, perform weddings in the bakery's chapel.

LUCKY OMEN
Sitting for a 2007 exam to become a firefighter, Alina Modoran, from Romania, wore her wedding dress. She had come straight from the church and had decided not to change out of her dress because she thought it would bring bad luck.

FUNERAL WEDDING
P. Sanjeevi Rajan of Port Klang, Malaysia, married his fiancée at his mother's funeral in 2007 to fulfil her dream of seeing him married.

DOG SUBSTITUTE
Dumped by her boyfriend two weeks before her wedding day, Emma Knight of Dorset, England, went ahead with the reception by wearing her $3,000 gown and dressing up her dog as the bridegroom.

NEVER A CROSS WORD!
When Aric Egmont of Cambridge, Massachusetts, wanted to propose to Jennie Bass, he decided to do so via a crossword puzzle. At his request, *The Boston Globe* Sunday magazine created a special puzzle where the crossword clues spelled out his proposal.

SERIAL HUSBAND
Sixty-eight-year-old Shehu Malami of Sokoto, Nigeria, has four wives and has been married a total of 201 times.

DUMMY RUN
When ventriloquists Eyvonne Carter and Valentine Vox married in Las Vegas, Nevada, their dummies—a baby doll and dog respectively—were present, too. The best man, maid of honor, bridesmaids, and ushers were all ventriloquists, accompanied by their dummies, and the ceremony was conducted by pastor Sheila Loosley—with her dummy, called Digger.

BALLOON WEDDING

Laura Dakin walked down the aisle at her wedding to Don Caldwell in 2006 wearing a dress made entirely out of twisted balloons. To add to the surreal nature of the Blue Hawaii-themed ceremony at the Viva Las Vegas Wedding Chapel in Las Vegas, Nevada, "Elvis" was on hand and the groom wore Hawaiian shorts. The couple met at a balloon-twisting convention and Caldwell (aka Buster Balloon) popped the question after stepping from a giant 6-ft (1.8-m) pink balloon.

At a wedding between two professional balloon twisters, it was only natural that even the bouquets were made of balloons.

It took the groom around eight hours to make the wedding dress from more than 200 white balloons. "I have worked on all sorts of projects before," said Don Caldwell, "but this was my first time making a life-sized, wearable dress."

23

SAUNA BIRTH
Until the 1920s, babies in Finland were often delivered in saunas, because the heat was thought to be beneficial in warding off infection for the newborn and the mother.

BANNED NAMES
Malaysian parents are issued a list of names that they are not permitted to give their children—including Hitler, smelly dog, hunchback, and 007.

SLEEPYHEAD DAY
July 27 is Sleepyhead Day in Finland, where the last person in the house to wake up is dragged out of bed and thrown into a lake or the sea.

SACRED METEORITE
Members of Oregon's Clackamas Indian tribe annually make a cross-country pilgrimage to visit the 15.5-ton Willamette Meteorite, which they consider sacred, at the American Museum of Natural History in New York City.

FROG RITUAL
In Rangpur Province, Bangladesh, villagers perform mock weddings with frogs in the belief that the ritual will bring rain.

CLEAN SWEEP
Italians moving into a new home use a broom to sweep away evil spirits and sprinkle salt in the corners of the house to purify it.

PATRIOTIC DINER
Customers at a West Virginia diner join waitress Judy Hawkins in singing the American national anthem every day at noon. Hawkins works at the Liberty Street Diner in Charles Town and encourages customers to stop eating and sing along to "The Star-Spangled Banner."

SPINSTER SEAT
Icelandic superstition says that an unmarried woman who sits at the corner of a table will not marry for at least another seven years.

COMB CAUTION
The Japanese believe it is bad luck to pick up a comb with its teeth facing your body.

Crying Sumo!

In a popular Japanese contest, two sumo wrestlers hold two toddlers facing each other and coax them to cry. The first child to burst into tears is declared the winner. Most of the children who participate are under one year old. Crying Sumo, as it is known, is designed to promote the child's health as, according to Japanese belief, crying is supposed to be good for babies.

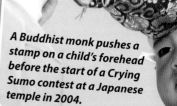

A Buddhist monk pushes a stamp on a child's forehead before the start of a Crying Sumo contest at a Japanese temple in 2004.

BALANCING ACT

Modern-day versions of traditional Japanese raftsmen, known as *kawanami*, ride on floating square logs during a festival in Tokyo. The custom dates back to the 17th century when agile Japanese lumberjacks were able to build rafts while standing on floating logs.

JUMPING DEVILS

At the El Colacho festival in Castrillo de Murcia, near Burgos, Spain, parents who want to protect their newborn babies from evil spirits lay them on the ground and allow grown men dressed as devils to jump over them.

SPITTING CONTEST

In a Sudanese marriage ritual, newlyweds have a milk spitting competition to decide who will become head of the household.

CAT CURSE

In some regions of France they believe that if a bachelor steps on a cat's tail, he will not find a wife for at least a year.

SWAN FOREBODING

To people in Scotland the sight of three swans flying together indicates that a national disaster is imminent.

TUSK CURRENCY

The 14 branches of the Tari Bunia Bank on Vanuatu's Pentecost Island have standard accounts, interest rates, and check books, and an unusual currency—pig's tusks. The tusks are paid into a customer's account, and the more they weigh, the greater their worth.

Jiang Musheng, 66, of China, has eaten a diet of live tree frogs and rats for the past 40 years. As a young man, he had suffered abdominal pains and coughing until an elderly villager prescribed the unusual remedy. After just one month of eating live frogs, the pains and coughing disappeared.

NORWEGIAN DELICACY

The local delicacy in the Norwegian town of Voss is smoked sheep's head. Nothing goes to waste except the bare bones of the skull as residents tuck in to the flesh of the entire head, including the sheep's eyeballs, tongue, and ears.

PRESERVED GIFT

A circle of friends has been handing around an old fruitcake as a Christmas present for more than 20 years. Christopher Linton-Smith, Steve Glum, and Tim Arnheim were friends at Stetson University, Florida, and started sending each other the $2.99 world-famous Claxton, Georgia, fruitcake as a joke in 1986. Each Christmas it is passed on to one of the group—even though none of them actually likes fruitcake.

ATE LENSES

Stopped by police for a breath test in 2007, a 19-year-old man from Ontario, Canada, took out his contact lenses and ate them—and then tried to eat his shirt and socks too.

Two students from the town of Swindon in Wiltshire, England, sat in a paddling pool in 2005 and ate dog food while fellow students pledged money to charity in return for covering them in baked beans, baking flour, and cornflakes.

ORGANIC RESTAURANT

Guolizhuang is China's first speciality penis restaurant. Every item on the menu at the Beijing diner is an animal's organ—yak, donkey, horse, dog, goat, deer, and ox. The luxury dish is Canadian seal's penis at $440. It has to be ordered in advance.

DESERT DIET

Eighty-year-old Ram Rati of Lucknow, India, eats 1 lb (450 g) of sand every day. She has been eating sand before each meal for the past 40 years and says it helps her to fight old age and stomach problems.

EDIBLE HEIRLOOM

A hot cross bun has been kept in a family for more than 100 years! Ever since 13-year-old Ada Herbert of Ipswich, England, died holding the bun in 1899, it has been passed down the family's generations. Amazingly, it has never gone moldy and the original cross is still visible.

Danny Partner of Los Angeles, California, used to eat 12 iceberg lettuces covered in chocolate sauce every day!

CARDBOARD BUNS

Steamed buns sold in a neighborhood of Beijing, China, are being made from cardboard! Although its use is illegal in foodstuffs, chopped cardboard, softened in caustic soda and enhanced with pork flavoring, is sometimes the main ingredient of the baozi buns.

ANTIQUE HAM

The same slab of ham has been on display at the Mecca restaurant in Raleigh, North Carolina, since 1937. The 25-lb (11-kg) ham was first acquired by the grandfather of the restaurant's current owner, Paul Dombalis, more than 70 years ago and has remained an uneaten favorite with customers ever since.

GRASS EATER

Gangaram, a man in Kanpur, India, has been eating more than 2 lb (900 g) of grass a day for many years. He says it gives him energy and that, although he can do without food, he cannot live without grass.

STEAMING RATS

Piping hot, cooked field rats are one of the dishes on offer at a wild game restaurant in Guangzhou, southern China.

BRAIN FOOD

This unusual-looking sandwich makes a regular appearance on the menu at the Hilltop Inn in Evansville, Indiana, even though it is made from deep-fried cow brains! Its origins are said to date back to a time when German and Dutch immigrants to southern Indiana wasted precious little of anything, especially when it came to animals slaughtered for food. Ketchup anyone?

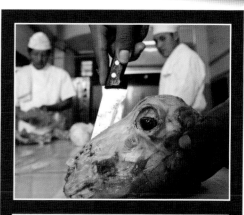

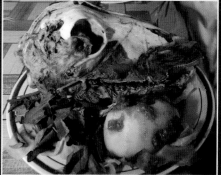

SHEEP SUPPER

Boiled sheep's head served on a bed of rice is the speciality of the Solar de las Cabecitas (House of the Little Heads), a restaurant in the Bolivian capital, La Paz. The dish originates from the Andean mining city of Oruro, where the salty highland pasture gives the lamb its particular flavor.

COSTLY COCKTAIL

Visitors to a nightclub in London, England, can buy a cocktail costing $70,000. The Flawless cocktail, which has to be ordered in advance, consists of a large measure of Louis XII cognac, half a bottle of Cristal Rose champagne, brown sugar, Angostura bitters, and a few flakes of 24-carat edible gold leaf. But what really makes the drink so expensive is at the bottom of the glass where, once you have supped the whole drink, there is a beautiful 11-carat white diamond ring.

CHOCOLATE FINGER

A man in Mainz, Germany, found part of a human finger in his chocolate bar. The fingertip, complete with nail, was right in the middle of the bar. A police officer said: "I suppose it went unnoticed because there were nuts in the chocolate and it was hard to tell the difference."

DINING TOMB

At the Lucky Hotel Restaurant in Ahmedabad, India, guests dine among the 22 tombs that remain from an ancient burial ground.

CHOC ART

Australian artist Sid Chidiac, who now lives in the Lebanon, paints with chocolate. He uses fine Belgian chocolate and food dye on an edible canvas to create portraits of, among others, John F. Kennedy, Oprah Winfrey, and Abraham Lincoln. Each painting takes him up to three days to complete and can last for several years if it is kept in the right conditions.

PAWS FOR THOUGHT

Chinese chef Wang Wei Min presents a plate of barbecued dogs' paws at a Chinese restaurant in Tokyo, Japan, in 2006. Apparently, Japanese diners are generally unaware that dog is served in Chinese restaurants in their country, but this dish would leave them in little doubt!

Renaissance man

Decorator Robert Burns has spent more than three years transforming the interior of his modest 1960s house in Brighton, England, into a Renaissance masterpiece. Using art books bought at rummage sales as his inspiration, he has faithfully reproduced the work of 15th-century Italian artists— mostly with emulsion paint from his local hardware store.

Robert has never been to Italy in his life, nor ever attended art school, but the books have enabled the 60-year-old father-of-four to re-create the beauty of Botticelli on his bedroom walls. A nativity scene with a

The façade of Robert's house conceals the treasures within.

trompe l'oeil (trick of the eye) gold frame dominates the dining room, while cameos of the Virgin Mary and other religious scenes are dotted throughout the house.

The hallway and lounge ceiling are adorned in a mass of fluffy clouds and blue sky, while the landing is decorated in an authentic marble effect.

Whereas Michelangelo, Leonardo da Vinci, and their contemporaries used a mixture of pigments and hundreds of egg yolks, Burns has to rely largely on household paint left over from his decorating jobs.

He adds to the Renaissance feel of the house whenever he is bored or between jobs, because it stops him going crazy waiting for the phone to ring.

He has always loved the Renaissance period and says it makes a refreshing change from his regular work. "Decorating can be a bit bland—one of my recent jobs was painting the inside of a factory with 53 liters of magnolia paint."

Ripley's ask

"**How did you discover your talent for painting?** I didn't know I could paint. I just went out and bought some brushes and paints and started painting the walls of our house. I had never painted anything before.

Have you had any formal training? My last art lesson was while I was in primary school.

Why in the Renaissance style? I started buying Renaissance art books at car boot sales and fell in love with Renaissance art and interiors. I have never seen any of these pictures or frescoes as they are in Italy.

Did you originally plan to do only one painting? My first painting in the house was on the upstairs landing. I painted a series of Lunettes over the door frames and it developed from there—I just kept adding to it.

What is your favorite piece of art and what room is it in? I am pleased with my effort in the dining room— 'The Madonna of the Chair' by Raphael and below that 'Virgin and Child' by Antoniazzo Romano.

What reactions have you had to your work? Most people are taken aback as it's not the interior you're expecting when going into a small house; but the reaction has always been favorable."

Robert applying the finishing touches to a Renaissance masterpiece in his home.

TAXI TRIP

Not wanting to travel by air for her vacation to Greece, 89-year-old Kathleen Searles of Suffolk, England, made the 4,000-mi (6,440-km) journey by taxi instead. Although she could have flown there for $120 and the taxi fare ended up costing her $4,000 and taking three days, she insisted that it was money well spent. Taxi driver Julian Delefortrie said: "When she asked me if I'd like to drive to Europe I replied that I would love to. I never expected her to say Greece!"

PORKY TRIBUTE

Rev. Bryan Taylor of Houston, Texas, created the Jeffrey Jerome Memorial Pig car in memory of Victoria Herbert's famous pet pig, Jeffrey Jerome. The pink auto has ears, a snout, and a curly tail.

SHUTTLE SHUFFLE

It takes more than six hours for NASA to move the U.S. space shuttle 3.4 mi (5.5 km) from its hangar to the launch pad.

HIGHWAY LANDING

In July 2007, a vintage airplane made an emergency landing on a Wisconsin highway. Pilot William J. Leff from Ohio, brought the 1946 North American T-6G plane down on the northbound lanes of U.S. Highway 41 near Fond du Lac County Airport. The only damage was to the plane's right wing when it hit a number of highway signs.

MONSTER SKATEBOARD

In 2007, students at Bay College, Michigan, built a skateboard measuring 31 ft (9.4 m) long and 8 ft (2.4 m) wide, and weighing 2,400 lb (1,090 kg). It can hold 28 people.

FLYING SAUCER

A sci-fi fan who admits he knows nothing about computers has spent more than 30 years building his own flying saucer in his garage. Alfie Carrington of Clinton, Michigan, has been putting the machine together using information from aviation books, and so far the project has cost him more than $60,000.

TINY ENGINE

Iqbal Ahmed of Nagpur, India, has built a working steam engine that weighs less than 0.07 oz (2 g). It stands just 0.267 in (6.8 mm) high and is 0.639 in (16.24 mm) long and, with steam generated by ⅓ fl oz (10 ml) water, the brass-constructed engine can run for about two minutes.

ROCKET ROBERT

In 1969, Achille J. St. Onge of Worcester, Massachusetts, sent a leather-bound miniature volume of Robert Goddard's autobiography on board *Apollo 11*, the first manned space flight to the Moon. Goddard was a pioneer of rocket building and his space-flown book, with pencil markings by Buzz Aldrin, was later valued at auction as being worth between $25,000 and $35,000.

HIGH RIDE

Brad Graham of Thunder Bay, Ontario, Canada, built a two-wheeled bicycle measuring 17 ft 10 in (5.5 m) tall. He rode it for 330 yd (300 m).

GIANT RABBIT

Designer Larry Fuente of Houston, Texas, attached a huge white rabbit to a Volkswagen Beetle to create his sinister-looking art car Rex Rabbit. Fuente had previously covered a pink Cadillac with a flock of flamingos.

SPELLING ERROR

Tobi Gutt of Germany traveled 8,000 mi (12,875 km) off-course after misspelling his destination city while buying an airline ticket. Instead of Sydney, Australia, he ended up in Sidney, Montana, United States.

SPEED CHASE

An 11-year-old girl was charged with drunk-driving in July 2007 after crashing while trying to escape her police pursuers at speeds of more than 100 mph (160 km/h). The girl gave police in Orange Beach, Alabama, the runaround for 8 mi (13 km) before they could catch her.

PLANE SPOTTERS

Nearly 100,000 people arrive daily at the new Suvarnabhumi Airport in Bangkok, Thailand—not to travel, but to sightsee and picnic!

SEVEN-SEATER BIKE

Eric Staller from Amsterdam, Netherlands, has invented a bicycle built for seven. The ConferenceBike, or CoBi, uses three motorcycle wheels and has seven seats in a circle. All seven riders can pedal, enabling the machine to reach speeds of up to 15 mph (24 km/h). One of the riders also takes charge of the steering wheel.

HANGING AROUND

Eelko Moorer of London, England, built a set of boots that allows him to hang upside down from safety rails in the subway. The boots have a slot in the heel that hooks over the carriage's handrail.

DOLPHIN CRAFT

New Zealander Rob Innes and Californian Dan Piazza have designed a watercraft that not only looks like a dolphin, it also behaves like a dolphin. The two-seater Seabreacher uses its 175 horsepower engine to surge through the waves, but because it is made of fiberglass, it is so light that it can fly 10 ft (3 m) in the air even at speeds of 15 mph (24 km/h). The advanced jet-ski is 15 ft (4.5 m) long and has a canopy similar to those seen on U.S. fighter jets.

Behind the exterior of John's modest home lies a replica of a 747 cockpit.

PLANE CRAZY

John Davis from Coventry, England, has spent eight years and $30,000 constructing an exact replica of a Boeing 747 cockpit in the spare bedroom of his house. The hi-tech simulator, which incorporates an autopilot system, weather radar, and engine sounds, was bought mainly over the Internet. To add to the illusion of real flight, he has erected a 6-ft (1.8-m) screen at the front of the cockpit showing panoramic views of places around the world, from the Alps to the skyline of New York. He even plays mock announcements, instructing passengers to fasten their seat belts to prepare themselves for takeoff.

John Davis studied photographs of a real Boeing 747-400 cockpit on aviation websites to make sure that the design for his home version was accurate.

ARMCHAIR RIDE

A company from DeMotte, Indiana, has designed a vehicle that enables couch potatoes to drive down the road without leaving the comfort of their armchair. Driven with a joystick and powered by either gasoline or electricity, Armchair Cruisers' range includes a Harley-Davidson chair that reaches speeds of 40 mph (64 km/h), does wheelies, and has an onboard cooler, and a two-seater sofa that can do two 360-degree turns inside an 8-sq-ft (0.74-sq-m) box. The chairs can even be customized with their own built-in stereo system.

GIRL RACER

Stephanie Beane of Grafton, Ohio, could roar around the track in a stock car at speeds of 80 mph (130 km/h)—at the age of ten. She made her stock-car debut at the Sandusky Speedway Motor-Sports Park in June 2007 and finished fifth in a field of 15, most of whom were adult men. She first got behind the wheel of a car when she was just two and started racing at four, learning to ride a go-kart before she could ride a bicycle. She was so successful—often winning trophies that were taller than she was—that she began signing autographs at age six... before she really knew how to write her name.

SUICIDE ATTACK

In August 2006, a large flock of shearwater birds bombarded a fishing boat off the coast of Alaska for unknown reasons, ramming suicidally against it for 30 minutes.

AUTHENTICITY SCAN

Zeng, an antique collector in Guangzhou, China, buys plane tickets so that he can go through the airport's X-ray scanners to verify the authenticity of artifacts that he carries with him!

VIRTUAL JOURNEY

Every Saturday in Delhi, India, around 40 passengers line up for boarding cards—for a plane that never takes off. For $4, Bahadur Chand Gupta offers people who cannot afford to fly the opportunity to experience air travel without ever leaving the ground. His Airbus 300 has only one wing, no lighting, and the toilets are out of order, but passengers happily buckle themselves in for their "virtual journey," watching safety demonstrations and listening to announcements while being waited on by flight attendants.

TOO WEAK

A 79-year-old woman from Norway was denied a driver's license renewal after losing an arm-wrestling match to her doctor.

FERRARI SALE

A red Ferrari Enzo with a top speed of 218 mph (350 km/h) was sold for more than $1 million on eBay's U.K. online auction site in 2006. Bidding started at the equivalent of $2.

TRAIN PUSH

In May 2007, a stalled commuter train in Bihar, India, was able to start again when hundreds of passengers got out and pushed!

SPOON VAN

Elmer Fleming of Columbia, South Carolina, has covered his Chevrolet pickup in kitchen utensils. He has riveted 1,480 spoons onto the bodywork.

FROZEN ORDEAL

An 11-year-old Russian stowaway survived an 800-mi (1,300-km) flight at temperatures of −58°F (−50°C) hidden in the wheel well of a Boeing 737. When Andrei Lyssov was finally discovered, many of his clothes were frozen to his body. He was then taken to a hospital where doctors treated him for frostbite.

BEE ESCAPE

Some 2,000 bees escaped and buzzed off when the truck carrying their hives overturned near Billings, Montana, in September 2007. The truck was hauling 465 beehives—holding nearly 13.7 million bees—from North Dakota to California, but luckily most of the bees stayed in their hives after the accident. As the weather cooled in the evening, the escaped bees returned to their hives, too.

SITTING TALL

Michael Mooney of Asheville, North Carolina, rides tall bikes for fun. He regularly rides bikes that are 6 ft (1.8 m) and 12 ft (3.6 m) tall, but in September 2007 he decided to go all the way by riding a bike that was an amazing 44 ft (13.4 m) tall—higher than a two-story house including the roof. He demonstrated it at the Lexington Avenue Arts and Fun Festival, and managed to pedal a few yards before the machine toppled over.

VINTAGE SALE

The world's oldest working car—the steam-powered La Marquise, built in France in 1884—was sold at auction in Pebble Beach, California, in 2007 for $3.5 million. The four-seater, which is fueled by coal, wood, and paper, takes about half an hour to work up enough steam to move.

FULL SPEED AHEAD

In January 1862, John Ericsson, a Swedish engineer, completed building an ironclad ship called the U.S.S. *Monitor* for the U.S. Navy in just 118 days.

VIKING VESSEL

An 11th-century Viking ship has been rebuilt from the wood of 300 oak trees. The 100-ft-long (30-m) *Sea Stallion* is held together by 7,000 iron nails and rivets. The original vessel sank south of Copenhagen, Denmark, in 1072 and lay there for nearly 900 years until excavated.

DRIVING BACKWARD

In October 2006, a man was stopped by police near the outback town of Kalgoorlie, Australia, after driving backward down a highway for 12 mi (20 km).

CUSTOM MADE

"Flat Out" was built in just three days, but at 22 in (56 cm) high is so low that at 6 ft 4 in (1.9 m), Andy Saunders can't fit into it. Consequently, his friend Jim Chalmers gets to drive it.

Andy Saunders spent six months modeling his Picasso Citroen on the work of the Spanish artist. The headlamps and indicators were inspired by Picasso's 1937 Portrait of Dora Maar. In spite of its misplaced features, the car is still capable of reaching 65 mph (105 km/h) but can be driven only during the day, when hand signals are permissible.

Andy Saunders specializes in taking old cars and turning them into something unrecognizable. The custom-car king, from Dorset, England, is a devotee of 1950s Americana, but gains inspiration from anywhere. He works at an auto center and spends his days studying the shape of windshields, headlamps, and other parts, which he then picks up from scrapyards to use on his latest projects. His crazy creations include a car that looks like a spaceship, a Citroen 2CV redesigned in the style of a Picasso painting *(left)*, and another vehicle that is just 22 in (56 cm) high *(above)*.

Page numbers in *italics* refer to illustrations

A

Ahmed, Arif (U.K.) 16
Ahmed, Iqbal (Ind) 30
airplanes
    cockpit replica in bedroom 31, *31*
    lands on highway 30
    stowaway survives low temperatures 33
    "virtual journey" on 32
    wrong destination 30
airport, sightseers 30
albino bison 11, *11*
antiques, authenticity verified 32
Antoniazzo Romano (Ita) 28
ants, bridge-making abilities 11
arm-wrestling, driver loses license 32
armchairs, motorized 32, *32*
Arnheim, Tim (U.S.A.) 26

B

babies
    born in saunas 24
    protecting from evil spirits 25, 25
bachelors, superstitions 25
bagel, very expensive 12, *12*
baked beans, students covered in 26
bakery, weddings in 23
balloons, wedding dress made of 23, *23*
balls, huge ball of popcorn 13
bananas
    banana-related accidents 13
    huge bunch of 16
bank, pig's tusk currency 25
barking, computer software translates 11
Bass, Jennie (U.S.A.) 23
Beane, Stephanie (U.S.A.) 32
Beaton, Rob (U.S.A.) 18
bees
    find landmines 10
    truck carrying overturns 33
Bevan, Kerry (U.K.) 22
bicycles
    for seven passengers 30
    very tall 30, 33
bionic hand 9, *9*
birds
    bombard fishing boat 32
    controlling flight of pigeons 10
    superstitions 25
bison, albino 11, *11*
Block, Lindsay (U.S.A.) 9, *9*

Blumenthal, Heston (U.K.) 13
Biwer, Renee (U.S.A.) 23
book, miniature book in space 30
boots, for hanging upside down in subway 30
Botticelli, Sandro (Ita) 28
Bradbury, Richard (U.K.) 18
brains, sandwich made of 27, *27*
bridesmaid, chicken as 23
bridges, ants make 11
brooms, sweeping away evil spirits 24
Browcott, Kris (U.K.) 18
Bruce, Stephen (U.S.A.) 13, *13*
burgers
    cheeseburger in can 15
    very expensive 12, *12*
Burns, Robert (U.K.) 28, *28–29*

C

caffeine, in soap 10
cakes
    enormous 17
    perpetual Christmas present 26
    replica of St. Paul's Cathedral, London 13
Caldwell, Don (U.S.A.) 23, *23*
Canida, Christy (U.S.A.) 10
cans
    cheeseburger in can 15
    refrigerator throws beer cans 15
cardboard, buns made of 26
carrots, first orange 12
cars
    child drunk-driver 30
    child stock car driver 32
    covered in kitchen utensils 32
    driver loses license after arm-wrestling match 32
    driving backwards 33
    huge rabbit on 30
    oldest working 33
    Picasso-inspired 33, *33*
    pig-shaped 30
    very expensive 32
    very low 33, *33*
Carter, Eyvonne (U.S.A.) 23
cats
    fearless mice 11
    fluorescent 10, *10*
    radio station for 10
    superstitions 25
cemeteries, restaurant in burial ground 27
chairs, motorized 32, *32*
Chalmers, Jim (U.K.) 33, *33*
Chaudhary, Phulram (Nep) 22
checkers, computer program 8
cheese, on Internet site 17
chicken
    as bridesmaid 23
    giant kebab 16
    giant pot of soup 16

chicken (*cont.*)
    mathematical ability 14, *14*
Chidiac, Sid (Aus) 27
chocolate
    diamond-encrusted 12, *12*
    eating lettuce covered in 26
    finger found in 27
    igloo made of 17
    painting with 27
    very expensive desserts 13, *13*
chopsticks, eating single grains of rice with 18
clothes
    bride wears wedding dress in exam 23
    discarded clothing on website 15
    family uses same wedding dress 22
    very long wedding dress 22, 22
    wedding dress made of balloons 23, *23*
cocktail, very expensive 27
coffee
    convict ordered to drink himself to death with 13
    drinking in every Starbucks 16–17, *17*
    giant cup of 17
    latte art 16, *16*
coins
    electrical charge from 15
    huge gold coin 15
computers
    checkers program 8
    mouse in mouse skin 10
contact lenses, man eats 26
Cornwell, John (U.S.A.) 15
corpses, get married 22
Crolla, Domenico (U.K.) 16
crossword, marriage proposal in 23
crying contest 24, *24*

D

D'Aubney, George (U.K.) 13
Dakin, Laura (U.S.A.) 23, *23*
Dantania, Sanjay (Ind) 22
Davies, Wayne (U.K.) 22
Davis, Jaina (U.S.A.) 6–7
Davis, John (U.K.) 31, *31*
Devipujak, Tulsi (Ind) 22
diamonds
    chocolate encrusted with 12, *12*
    turning peanut butter into 14
    very expensive cocktail 27
divorce, man gives ring finger to ex-wife 23
dog food, students eat 26
dog, man marries 22
dogs
    barbecued dogs' paws 27, *27*
    computer software translates barks 11

dogs (*cont.*)
    resuscitating 11
dolphin jet-ski 30, *30*
Dombalis, Paul (U.S.A.) 26
drunk-driving child 30

E

eBay, imaginary friend sold on 14
eggs
    boiled with lightbulbs 10
    giant omelette 13
    self-timing boiled eggs 15, *15*
Egmont, Aric (U.S.A.) 23
electricity, in sweat 15
electrons, weight of in Internet 8
Elgar, Edward (U.K.) 8
Elizabeth II, Queen of England 15
Enters, Valerie (U.S.A.) 18
Ericsson, John (Swe) 33
evil spirits
    protecting babies from 25, 25
    sweeping away 24
exam, bride wears wedding dress in 23
explosives, bees find landmines 10
eye socket, needle in 9

F

Fanti, Marco (Ita) 17
finger
    found in chocolate bar 27
    man gives ring finger to ex-wife 23
fire, riding horses through 20, *20–21*
fish, restaurant buys expensive "lucky" fish 17
fish hook, eaten in restaurant 18
fishing boat, bombarded by birds 32
Fleming, Elmer (U.S.A.) 32
fluorescent cats 10, *10*
fly, robotic 8
flying saucer, homemade 30
food
    long-lived 26
    speed-eating 18
    very expensive 12, *12*, 13, *13*, 16
football, specially flavored soda 18
Francis, Steve (U.S.A.) 16
frogs
    eating 26, 17
    mock weddings with 24
    transparent 11, *11*
fudge, enormous slab of 12
Fuente, Larry (U.S.A.) 30
funeral, wedding at 23

G

Gangaram (Ind) 26
geckos, super-sticky glue 10
Gillette, King Camp (U.S.A.) 9

gingerbread houses 18, *18–19*
glue, super-sticky material 10
Glum, Steve (U.S.A.) 26
goat's milk, nerve gas antidote 10
Goddard, Robert (U.S.A.) 30
gold
   huge coin 15
   very expensive cocktail 27
   very expensive dessert 13, *13*
golf cart, converted to snowplow 15
Graham, Brad (Can) 30
grass, eating 26
Gupta, Bahadur Chand (Ind) 32
Gustav III, King of Sweden 13
Gutt, Tobi (Ger) 30

H

ham, long-lived 26
hands
   bionic 9, *9*
   finger found in chocolate bar 27
Hawkins, Judy (U.S.A.) 24
heads, eating sheep's 26, 27, *27*
Heeman, Rudy (Nzl) 14, *14*
Herbert, Ada (U.K.) 26
Herbert, Victoria (U.S.A.) 30
horses, riding through fire 20, *20–21*
hospital-themed restaurant 17, *17*
hot cross bun, long-lived 26
houses
   gingerbread 18, *18–19*
   sweeping away evil spirits 24
hovercraft, flying 14, *14*
Howard, Patricia (U.S.A.) 18

I

ice cream
   enormous sundae 16
   unusual flavors 19, *19*
igloo, chocolate 17
Innes, Rob (Nzl) 30, *30*
Internet
   cheese matures on 16
   fast surfing 14
   weight of electrons and protons in 8
iPod, served with restaurant meal 13

J

Janus, Tim (U.S.A.) 18
jet-ski, dolphin 30, *30*
Jiang Musheng (Chn) 26
Johnson, Levi (U.S.A.) 18

K

kebab, giant 16
Kennedy, John F. (U.S.A.) 27
kitchen utensils, car covered in 32
Knight, Emma (U.K.) 23
Kyzer, Nancy (U.S.A.) 19

L

Laidre, Kristin (U.S.A.) 10
landmines, bees find 10
latte art 16, *16*
Lauer, Bill (U.S.A.) 15
laughing, weight loss with 11
Leff, William J. (U.S.A.) 30
Leonardo da Vinci (Ita) 28
lettuces, eating covered in chocolate 26
lie detector, in sunglasses 15
lightbulbs, boiling eggs with 10
Lincoln, Abraham (U.S.A.) 27
Linton-Smith, Christopher (U.S.A.) 26
Liu Ye (Chn) 22
Logan, James Harvey (U.S.A.) 17
loganberries 17
logs, standing on floating 25, *25*
Loosley, Sheila (U.S.A.) 23
Lothberg, Sigbritt (Swe) 14
lychee, very expensive 13, *13*
Lyssov, Andrei (Rus) 33

M

Ma Yanjun (Chn) 15
MacCallister, Trish (U.S.A.) 18
Malami, Shehu (Nga) 23
marriage
   superstitions 24
   proposal in crossword 23
math, chicken's ability 14, *14*
Mecier, Jason (U.S.A.) 6–7, *6–7*
meteorite, pilgrimage to 24
mice
   computer mouse in skin of 10
   fearless 11
Michelangelo (Ita) 28
Middleton, Charlotte (U.K.) 22
milk spitting competition 25
mine, wedding in 22
missing people, search for 15, *15*
money, pig's tusks as currency 25
Mooney, Michael (U.S.A.) 33
Moorer, Eelko (U.K.) 30
Morris, Terry (U.S.A.) 23
mosaic, made from pencils 6–7, *6–7*
mussels, super-sticky glue 10

N

names, prohibited in Malaysia 24
nanotechnology, copy of Rodin's *The Thinker* 8
narwhals, scientific instruments strapped to 10
needle, in eye socket 9
nerve gas antidote, in goat's milk 10
Newton, Sir Isaac (U.K.) 9
nuclear reactor, home-made 11

O

oceans, narwhals help researcher 10

Olson, Thiago (U.S.A.) 11
omelette, giant 13
Osborne, Jessica (U.S.A.) 18

P

paintings
   house full of Renaissance 28, *28–29*
   latte art 16, *16*
   with chocolate 27
pajamas, temperature-controlled 15
pancakes, squirrel 18
Partner, Danny (U.S.A.) 26
peanut butter, turning into diamonds 14
pencils, mosaic made from 6–7, *6–7*
penis restaurant 26
Piazza, Dan (U.S.A.) 30, *30*
Picasso, Pablo (Spa) 33, *33*
pig, car shaped like 30
pigeons, controlling flight of 10
pigs, tusks as currency 25
Pilarz, Virginia (U.S.A.) 19
pilgrimage, to meteorite 24
pizzas
   enormous 18
   very expensive 16
plants, ask for water by telephone 9
popcorn
   huge ball of 13
   making huge quantity of 18
poppadums, stacking 18
Portnoy, Rich and Andra (U.S.A.) 18
potato, man knocked out with 13
Prisbrey, Grandma (U.S.A.) 7

R

rabbit, huge model on car 30
radio station, for cats 10
Rajan, P. Sanjeevi (Mal) 23
Raphael (Ita) 28
Rati, Ram (Ind) 26
rats
   eating 26, *26*
   giant 11
razor, slow sales for safety razor 9
refrigerator, throws beer cans 15
restaurants
   in ancient burial ground 27
   expensive "lucky" fish 17
   hospital-themed 17, *17*
   iPod served with meal 13
   penis restaurant 26
   "The Star-Spangled Banner" sung at 24
   transatlantic takeout 16
   $10,000 tip 18
Rhymes, Simon (U.K.) 10

rice
   eating single grains with chopsticks 18
   sushi on single grain of 12
roads, airplane lands on highway 30
robots
   fly 8
   personal "clone" 8, *8*
   rescues wounded soldiers 9
   violin player 8, *8*
   waiter 15
rocket belts, annual convention 8
rodents, giant 11
Rodin, Auguste (Fra) 8
Rogiani, Mike (Can) 16
Rosen, Nohl (U.S.A.) 10

S

St. Onge, Achille J. (U.S.A.) 30
St. Paul's Cathedral, London, fruitcake replica of 13
salt, purifying houses with 24
sand, eating 26
sandwich, made of brains 27, *27*
saunas, babies delivered in 24
Saunders, Andy (U.K.) 33, *33*
Searles, Kathleen (U.K.) 30
sheep's heads, eating 26, 27, *27*
ships
   U.S.S. *Monitor* built very quickly 33
   Viking ship rebuilt 33
shirt, man tries to eat 26
shoes
   retractable heels 15
   vacuum cleaner in 8
skateboard, enormous 30
sleep
   temperature-controlled pajamas 15
   Sleepyhead Day 24
snowplow, golf cart converted to 15
soap, caffeine in 10
socks, missing 14
soda, football-flavored 18
sofas, motorized 32, *32*
soldiers, robot to rescue wounded 9
sorbets, unusual flavors 19, *19*
soup, giant pot of 16
space shuttle, journey to launch pad 30
space travel, miniature book on Apollo mission 30
squirrel pancakes 18
Staller, Eric (Nld) 30
Starbucks, man drinks coffee in every 16–17, *17*
"The Star-Spangled Banner", sung at restaurant 24
steam engine, minute 30
stock cars, child driver 32

subway, boots for hanging upside
    down in 30
sumo wrestlers, crying contest
    24, 24
sunglasses, lie detector in 15
sushi, on single grain of rice 12
swans, superstitions 25
sweat, electrical charge from 15

T

Tabasco® sauce, drinking 18
taxi, long journey by 30
Taylor, Rev. Bryan (U.S.A.) 30
tea bag, enormous 16
telephones
    plants ask for water by 9
    tribe chants ringtones 15
television, same size as coin 8
Thanksgiving meal, speed-eating
    18
Tie Guangju (Chn) 22, 22
tip, $10,000 18
toilets, multi-tasking 15
trains, pushed by passengers 32
trees, marriage ceremony 23
truffles, cost of 12, 18
Tujague, Frank (U.S.A.) 12
turkey, giant 18

V

vacuum cleaner, in shoes 8
ventriloquists, wedding 23
violins, robot player 8, 8
Vox, Valentine (U.S.A.) 23

W

waiter, robotic 15
waitress, $10,000 tip 18
Wang Wei Min (Chn) 27, 27
Washington, George (U.S.A.) 12
water, solar heated 15

weddings
    in bakery chapel 23
    bride marries corpse 22
    bride wears wedding dress in
        exam 23
    chicken as bridesmaid 23
    dress made of balloons 23, 23
    family uses same dress 22
    at funeral 23
    jilted bride holds reception 23
    man marries dog 22
    man marries himself 22
    milk spitting competition 25
    much-married groom 23
    in slate mine 22
    trees marry 23
    of ventriloquists 23
    very long dress 22, 22
    on window-cleaning platforms
        22, 22
    with frogs 24
weight loss
    weight-loss pill 9
    with laughing 11
Weinsrein, Noah (U.S.A.) 10
whiskey, distillery run by George
    Washington 12
Willamette Meteorite 24
window cleaners, married on
    work platforms 22, 22
Winfrey, Oprah (U.S.A.) 27
Winter (U.S.A.) 16–17, 16

Z

Zeng (Chn) 32
Zou Renti (Chn) 8, 8

ACKNOWLEDGMENTS

COVER (l) Dan Piazza, (t/r) Robert Burns of Brighton; BACK COVER www.Armchaircruisers.com; 4 Dan Piazza; 6–7 Richard Barnes www.jasonmecier.com; (t) Katsumi Kasahara/AP/PA Photos, (b) Reuters/Jason Lee; 9 Brandi Simons/Getty Images; 10 Choi Byung-kil/AP/PA Photos; 11 (t) John Steiner, (b) Masayuki Sumida/AP/PA Photos; 12 (t) Reuters/Yuriko Nakao, (r) Reuters/Jacob Silberberg, (l) Reuters/Kiyoshi Ota; 13 (t) Reuters/Chip East, (b) Reuters/China Photos; 14 (t) Barcroft Media, (b) ChinaFotoPress/Photocome/PA Photos; 15 (t) Allan Bovill/Strathclyde Police/PA Wire/PA Photos, (b) Rex Features; 16 (t/c, t/r) N Connolly/Newspix/Rex Features; 16–17 (b) Winter; 17 (t/l, t/r) Reuters/Richard Chung; 18 Berkson Photography; 19 (t) Paul Cooper/Rex Features, (b) Berkson Photography; 20–21 Jasper Juinen/Getty Images; 22 (t) ChinaFotoPress/Photocome/PA Photos, (b) AP/PA Photos; 23 Don and Laura Caldwell www.AcmeBalloon.com; 24 Koichi Kamoshida/Getty Images; 25 (t) Kazuhiro Nogi/AFP/Getty Images, (b) Denis Doyle/Getty Images; 26 Reuters/China Photos; 27 (t/l) Daniel R. Patmore/AP/PA Photos, (t/r, c/r) Reuters/David Mercado, (b) Toru Yamanaka/AFP/Getty Images; 28–29 Robert Burns of Brighton; 30 Dan Piazza; 31 David Burner/Rex Features; 32 www.Armchaircruisers.com; 33 Phil Yeomans/Rex Features

Key: t = top, b = bottom, c = center, l = left, r = right, sp = single page, dp = double page

All other photos are from Ripley Entertainment Inc.

Every attempt has been made to acknowledge correctly and contact copyright holders and we apologize in advance for any unintentional errors or omissions, which will be corrected in future editions.